Be, Heal, Live

by

Pam Denton, DC and Sarah Kaczor

Acknowledgements

We'd like to extend our heartfelt gratitude and sincere appreciation to the many friends and family members who have supported this project since it first appeared as twinkles in our eyes. We want to especially thank and honor our business partner, Randy, who dedicated himself to our process and trusted in a successful outcome. As we've said all along, you wrote this book and program.

Thank You.

Contents

Introduction

You're tired. You're confused. You've hit bottom. You are suffering and at the end of your rope. Or, you're numb. You feel lifeless and your senses are deadened. In any case, you don't know what to do, where to go, or who to trust—but you know something has to shift.

You are ready to do whatever it takes to turn your life around.

You have reached the crisis point—
the place where deep change begins.

Whether your crisis stems from illness, depression, bereavement, poverty, an accident, or simply an abiding sense that something is amiss, it is important. What you are feeling right now is essential to your life experience.

Why? Because it will lead you toward the happiness and fulfillment you crave.

Your suffering is here to help you.

We at Seven Petals Wellness have helped countless clients emerge from the darkness severe suffering into the light of hope, belief, and positive creation.

We are here to help you see the light at the end of the tunnel. We will help you go *through* the tunnel and emerge refreshed.

We are not going to counsel you to avoid your crisis, because it is a sacred aspect of your path here on earth. Your crisis is not life working against you. It is life working *with* you.

Your crisis is sacred.

Your crisis is your spirit's way of awakening you to the fact that something needs to shift. It works like this: When you are in crisis, your normal defenses are down. This means you are very close to the deepest and most sacred parts of yourself.

From this sacred place, your spirit can offer you the wisdom to profoundly shift the direction of your life toward health, well-being, abundance, and lasting happiness.

This shift need not be difficult. It doesn't take a lot of *doing*. It takes only two things: a readiness for a shift to happen, and a willingness to commit to your personal growth.

Shifting your life doesn't mean changing who you are.

It means deepening your connection with the sacred core of yourself, the wise part of you that knows exactly what you need to be happy and fulfilled.

We are here to guide you through a simple formula that will take you from crisis to calm, from chaos to clarity, from dead to alive. We know it works because we have used it with people undergoing all types of crisis, mild to severe.

Using the crisis formula has allowed us to witness people shift their lives from the paralysis of crisis to positive action that aligns with life purpose. We now invite you to partake of the formula's profound and lasting benefits.

To help you shift, this book is divided into three sections: **Be, Heal, and Live.** Each section has two chapters designed to help you reap the hidden gifts of your crisis and move into a new level of self-love and life fulfillment.

Following the simple practices in each chapter will help you move out of the negative, stagnant, toxic energy of suffering into the positive, dynamic, and exciting energy of living authentically.

Right now, all you need to do is be in the experience of your crisis. We will help you do that in the first part of the book. Being where you are is the place to begin. We do not ask that you try to feel better or negate the importance of the crisis you are undergoing. Here is where it all begins.

Crisis is defined as a turning point. You are at that point, and from here you have the ability to shift your life toward what you most deeply desire.

You can heal your pain and find happiness.

Starting here, in the depth of crisis, you have the power to turn your life around. You don't have to know yet how that will happen or how it will look. This book will provide the support and help you need to discover hidden resources in yourself that you may not have dreamed existed.

You have already begun.

be

Chapter One

Be Silent

In your sacred place of crisis, silence and contemplation are your greatest allies. You need time to be able to dive into the heart of your crisis and really *feel* it. Your suffering has gifts for you, and it is your right and privilege to go inward and receive them.

Does this sound uncomfortable to you?

If it does, it's because our culture does not place great value on going inward. We are constantly looking outside ourselves for answers, entertainment, and distractions. Yet, as you may have begun to sense, this inner journey is essential for healing.

The first step is connecting to the reality of your suffering. When you delve into your experience, you have the opportunity to emerge refreshed. If, on the other hand, you avoid your feelings by staying busy, eating, drinking, watching TV, or working, you are neglecting that sacred part of yourself that is aching to accept what life is offering.

Your crisis is an offering—a spiritual push toward finding what is authentic for you. Your crisis offers you the opportunity to deepen your experience of life and discover what you really want. This can be revealed to you by connecting with spirit through silence.

Crisis is life's way of activating your connection to spirit.

How you define spirit is up to you. You might think of it as God, Goddess, nature, the universe, or the divine. Whatever you call it, spirit is that part of you that carries a higher wisdom or knowingness. Spirit is what awakened you to the fact that something needed to change by creating a crisis in your life.

You may well wonder, "Why did it take such a catastrophe to for me to awaken? Why couldn't it have been gentler?"

Think about how busy you are in everyday life. It is possible that spirit tried some subtle ways to invite you to shift your life, but you either didn't notice the signs or decided to get to it later. It's easy to get so caught up in the daily round of appointments and commitments that spirit has to take drastic action—or even a series of drastic actions—before you slow down enough to listen.

Listening to spirit's messages often begins when you hit bottom. That low point feels really terrible, yet it is when spirit is connecting with you most strongly. When you can be silent and listen, spirit helps you recognize that you need to do something different.

*Silence is essential for dealing with the emotional
and physical upheaval of crisis.*

Spirit has caused a crisis to slow you down and help you connect with yourself. Rest and quietude are imperative for you right now. Like a pure spring in the heart of a forest, silence refreshes you from a clean place of stillness. From this place, you will be able to reflect differently upon your circumstances.

To honor this sacred opportunity, find a place of inner silence.

Place your hands on your heart and breathe.

That is all you need to do. *Place your hands on your heart, and breathe.*

Breathing is the simplest thing you can do in life, isn't it? Usually, it happens without even thinking about it. When you consciously connect to your breath, you can reunite with the sensation of simplicity.

Simplicity is important for you right now. In times of crisis, life can seem very complicated. Putting conscious attention to breathing reconnects you to the valuable quality of simplicity. Being in the simplicity of breath offers a welcome respite from life's complexity, as well as the opportunity to gain perspective on your situation.

When you breathe in the midst of conflict, you can eliminate confusion. When you are breathing, that is all you need to think about. Your mind, body, and emotions all have a chance to rest, and you emerge refreshed. Breath is the anchor that connects you to the sacred parts of you—the life-giving purity of spirit.

Take a moment now to begin this practice of breathing. Place your hands palm over palm on your heart and breathe deeply, three full cycles of inhale and exhale. Continue to breathe, closing your eyes. As you breathe:

Listen to the wavelike sound of your breath.

Listen for the silence.

Let your breath create a deep well of silence in you—a place of peace, where the inner and outer chaos can slow to a stop. Imagine the chaos lifting off of you like a weight being released. As it lifts, settle into your body.

Sense your hands on your heart.

Sense your heartbeat under your hands.

Sense the rise and fall of your chest as you breathe.

Sense the position of your body.

Sense your feet.

As you continue to breathe and settle into your body, you might feel tears well up. Let them gather and fall freely in a cleansing stream. Don't try to stifle or contain your tears. Let them fall until they are finished.

Next, for healing, curl into the healing position of **hug the rock** or the comforting posture called **child's pose.**

Hug the Rock

<u>Purpose</u>: To calm, comfort and nurture; to provide self-care with gentleness and support.

Sit back on your heels, or if it is more comfortable, sit in a chair with your feet on the floor. Cross your arms across your chest and place your hands on opposite shoulders. Hugging yourself, exhale and rock forward; inhale and rock backward.

Child's Pose

Purpose: To access stability, strength, stillness, rest, and peace.

Sit back on your heels or sit in a chair. Roll your abdomen down over your thighs then gently drop your forehead and nose to the floor. Place your arms alongside your legs, palms up. Breathe deeply, pushing your breath into the abdomen, pelvis, and tailbone.

Stay in the posture as long as you need to. You will know when you are finished. Give yourself some time to come back into the room and prepare yourself for re-entering the world.

You now have a tool you can use to help yourself experience your crisis safely. This tool of creating silence through breathing will connect you to spirit and help you through your day.

Create a practice of silence.

Start to find pockets of silence whenever possible. Become a detective and seek those places where you can have a moment alone to breathe. It could be in your car, in a bathroom stall or deserted stairwell at work, or in a relatively quiet and unoccupied space at home—in the garage, the bathroom, the attic, or in bed.

Any time you place your hands on your heart and breathe, you are honoring spirit's crisis offering. This practice will connect you to silence and give you a respite from the chaos around you. The simplicity of this practice will help you clear your mind, heart, and spirit.

When you go into silence, you connect to the pure, healing essence of spirit. When you connect to spirit, you connect to the sacred part of you that wants to heal.

Chapter Two

Be Real

"Am I crazy?"

This is the number one question people in crisis ask when they come to us for help. They are often in such distress, and feel so out of control, that they fear they're losing their mind. This fear tends to be exacerbated by the other people in their lives who can't understand the crisis and therefore react negatively.

If the question "Am I crazy?" has come up for you, the answer is NO.

You are not crazy.

You are undergoing a profound process of shift, one that will propel you further forward than you have ever imagined. You will look back at this point in your life as one of the most profound and transformational times you ever experienced.

However, the outside world might not understand or align with what you are going through right now. People want life to be easy, and it is difficult for them to see someone they love suffer. Automatically, they want to stop your crisis, taking away your pain and suffering as a means of support. What they may not understand is that their "help" actually hinders your progression toward healing and resolution.

That's why you need to protect yourself during this time of crisis. No matter how good people's intentions in trying to help you, it is all too easy for them to negate the importance of your experience by offering advice or questioning your process. Be discerning about sharing what you are going through.

Advice from questioning or doubting bystanders can halt your healing. Certainly, you must seek advice from a health professional if you are in need of medical or psychiatric attention. Otherwise, share your crisis only with people you are sure will show support by simply listening. Or you may choose not to share your crisis with anyone.

Whether or not you share your experience with anyone, the safest and most powerful way to express what you are going through is by keeping a private journal.

Journaling is like sharing your deepest thoughts and emotions with a trusted friend—one who will always support you and never offer unwanted advice or opinions. Journaling allows you to express yourself freely, without fear or restrictions. Journaling is a safe, healing way to write your story.

Your story is important.

What happened to cause this crisis? How do you feel? What thoughts are going through your mind? What is your day like? All these are aspects of your story, and your story is important. Writing about your story can help you…

- Release the thoughts and feelings surrounding your situation

- Illuminate the truth of where you are

- Work through difficult emotions

- Express yourself freely

- Trust that you will be okay

Find a notebook or sketch pad that pleases you and write in it whenever you feel like you need validation for your experience or have a thought to share. Write about your nighttime dreams, your everyday interactions, your suffering, your intentions, your desires, your pain, or whatever you feel called to write.

Don't censor yourself. Your writing doesn't have to be sequential, sound profound, or make sense. You don't have to spell correctly or use proper grammar. You can jot down one word or let a torrent of sentences pour out. You can draw pictures, doodle, or paste in photographs.

Your journal is a healing tool for *you*. It is your ally and companion. It will help you heal your crisis by allowing you a forum for unlimited self-expression. It provides a rich ground for releasing emotion and gaining insight, both now and later. Your journal will be an essential tool as you connect with your crisis and honor it as sacred. Keep it close by you whenever possible. It is your direct line to spirit.

In your journal, you will cultivate the art of **being real.**

Being real means expressing the truth
of the moment, no matter what it is.

Your emotions want expression. If they are repressed or denied, they will fester and cause further disease or depression. Being real is being one hundred percent present in your heartfelt truth, *right now*—even if what is true changes a moment later.

Being real means letting go of self-blame or self-judgment. There is no right or wrong way to feel. You could feel ten different things in one moment, or feel one way very strongly then feel its opposite just as strongly. Being real is simply expressing the truth of your emotions.

When you allow yourself to express the truth of your emotions, you instantly begin to heal. Expressing them helps them dissipate and lose their hold over you. This doesn't mean spilling your emotions all over other people. Your journal is the perfect place to express your truth without hurting anyone or inviting damaging repercussions.

*   *   *

To begin writing your story, stimulate the words through movement by doing the following exercises.

Swirl

Purpose: To move from internal to external; to become an eye of peace amid the swirling storm of crisis.

Sit on the floor cross-legged, or in a chair with your feet on the floor. Place your hands on your knees. Inhale and lift through the spine and the crown of your head. Exhale, rolling your torso forward over your right knee, center, then over your left knee. Inhale, returning to the beginning position. Repeat six to ten times.

Pump

<u>Purpose</u>: To release stored or blocked energy or emotions.

Sit on your heels, or in a chair with your feet on the floor. Let your belly be soft and extended. Inhale with relaxed belly then exhale actively, swiftly pulling up and in with your abdominal muscles. Repeat ten to twenty times.

Now that you have gotten some motion going in your body, it is time to access the words. Imagine that all the unexpressed words in your life have been cluttering you up inside, keeping you mired in crisis and unable to relax and be. Now, it is time to release the words. To get the words started, do the "stomach pump" exercise. Imagine that as you do the pump, the words will literally vomit out of you, splattering on the page.

Do not do this exercise on a full stomach!

Write

Then, ask yourself the following questions and write the answers in your journal. Write whatever comes up without censoring yourself. Let the words come out just the way the do. Don't try to organize your thoughts or put things in chronological order.

What is the reality of my situation right now?

Where am I today?

After you have written all you have to say right now, put down your pen, sit back, and congratulate yourself for being real. You have made a connection with yourself, and in the truth of this connection is your bridge to healing. Let yourself sit with this new connection by returning to a state of Be.

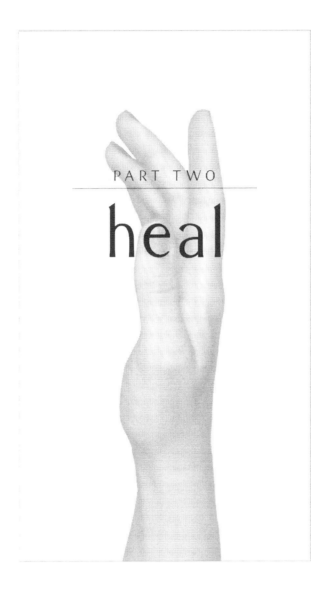

PART TWO

heal

Chapter Three

Feel, Trust, Witness

How is it to simply let yourself Be in your crisis?

Using the tools of breathing and journaling, you can choose to stay in the stage of Be for as long as you need to. As you continue to practice and use your new tools, you will eventually feel a desire to come up for air—to resurface from your crisis. This desire means you are ready to move into the next stage: healing.

Healing begins with three basic steps: **Feel, trust,** and **witness**. These steps will help you connect with your crisis as a gateway to a new and improved way of life. It doesn't mean negating your suffering; rather, your suffering provides the impetus to seek health and well-being. Your suffering can lead you to the life-giving truth hidden in the depths of your crisis. Let your suffering be your guide, leading you forward to find your inner wisdom. Like the calm after a storm, your wisdom will surface for you to capture.

Healing is finding life.

You can find out if you are ready for the healing stage of crisis by gently asking yourself, **"Can I do this now?"** You will know the answer is yes if you feel an inner push to move into the healing stage.

Next, place your hands on your heart and say, **"I am able to move forward."** See if the statement feels good and right in your heart. If it doesn't, you might need to stay in Be a bit longer. If it does, you are ready to use your crisis as a springboard, or bridge, to a new state of health and well-being.

The impetus to heal may have already arrived. If you know you are ready to begin healing today, read on. If not, stay in the Be stage and trust that your natural timing will reveal itself. Only *you* know when you are ready to move out of being and into healing. Don't worry about how you will know. Connecting to your breath and expressing yourself in your journal will allow you to follow what is right for you.

Feel

Whatever form your crisis has taken until now, you have been in a state of physical, emotional, and mental *dis-ease*. In such a state, your body's natural healing function is suppressed to an extreme extent. This suppression is so powerful that it saps your life force—your will to live. That's why you feel tired, numb, overwhelmed, and sometimes unable to deal with simple everyday tasks.

This inertia is not a permanent state. It is your body's way of telling you that something needs to change. Your dis-ease is your body speaking to you, and your symptoms are a wake-up call. To begin healing, listen to what they are saying.

At the most basic level, the symptoms are saying, "Feel me! Express me!" That's because buried beneath the surface of your crisis are layers of stifled self-expression. When repressed, feelings build up inside you and literally weigh you down, sapping your life force. So what can you do to counteract this destructive process? It's simple: *feel what you feel.* Healing begins with supporting and expressing your feelings instead of suppressing them. When you can to feel your crisis from the inside out, you will begin to heal.

You must feel to heal.

Supporting your feelings allows you to begin releasing the suppression that led to your crisis. When you begin to express the feelings of your crisis, the wake-up call of your symptoms will begin to dissipate. This is where the path toward a happy, fulfilling life begins.

To connect with your feelings, take the following steps.

- Use your journal as a tool for expressing your feelings. Take out your journal several times a day and write, "I feel…"
- Before you go to bed or first thing in the morning, write about your feelings in more detail, as expressively as possible. Alternatively, you could draw or cut and paste pictures that describe your feelings.
- Begin to define the emotions associated with where you are, right now.
- Breathe into these emotions and let them Be part of your experience.
- Be real.

Trust

As you begin to **feel** your crisis from the inside out, be prepared for an emotional roller coaster. It is common to experience an extreme high, or energized period, that plummets without warning into old feelings of pain or depression. That's because healing does not happen on a straight trajectory. It tends to take you on a bumpy ride as you release suppressed feelings.

At this point, it is essential to **trust** the process of healing. The process has its own intelligence, and it is working even when things seem chaotic. Be assured that the emotional and physical roller coaster is a healthy part of the healing process.

During this time, it may seem as if things are not moving forward. You may have a sinking sense that you have been here before. You might get sick or have flu-like symptoms. This emotional and physical revisiting of your crisis is a good sign. Just as a cut will hurt or itch as it begins to heal, you will feel discomfort as healing starts to happen.

You may go through several cycles of healing as you uncover layers of suppressed feelings. Your body and emotions will experience layers of healing that may feel repetitive. Look for subtle signs of shift, and trust that each layer is bringing you closer to completion of your crisis. It is crucial to trust that you *are* moving forward. While you are working the steps of this program, you will experience relief within a day or two. Although may be difficult to really have to feel what you are going through, keep going. You are worth it. Let trust be your companion.

Trust the process.

In addition to supporting your healing on an emotional level, it is important to support yourself physically. This doesn't have to take a lot of effort, since your body is already intrinsically equipped for survival. Simply **trust** your body's instincts guide you toward what you need. Trust that you will automatically reach out for the necessary nourishment and nurturing.

Take the following simple steps to increase your life force and support your healing crisis.

- **Rest.** Sleep as much as possible, and include rest breaks in your schedule. If resting requires taking time off, allow yourself the time. Sleep is where the body restores itself, so let sleep support you in healing.

- **Hydrate.** Buy filtered water, or use a filter at home so your water is free of toxins. Carry water with you and respond consistently to your instinctual urge to drink. Water fortified with electrolytes, such as Vitamin Water, is especially good for keeping your energy balanced.

- **Eat.** Let your body lead you to the food you need to nourish yourself. Lean toward healthy, fresh foods if possible—but if you are drawn to unhealthy foods, allow yourself to eat them for energy. However, do not force yourself to eat if you have no appetite, because the digestive process can draw important healing energy away from your emotional and spiritual healing process. If you find yourself in a stage of under-eating or overeating, ride it out. As you release suppressed feelings, your body will respond and regulate what you put in your system.

In addition to this basic healing support, you may want to seek support from a trusted practitioner who can help guide your physical and emotional process. Be selective about who you see. Good choices are naturopathic doctors, homeopathic doctors, Doctors of Oriental Medicine, counselors, Reiki practitioners, acupuncturists, and chiropractors.

Even if you seek outside help, it is essential to cultivate trust in your body's innate knowledge of what you need. No matter who is giving you advice, trust yourself above all others. Always follow your instincts if they are different from what someone else tells you to do. If you get advice that doesn't seem to fit where you are right now, don't reject it out of hand; simply put it aside for later.

If you find yourself saying "I'm fine," take note. "I'm fine" is a wall you put up to reject support in the healing process. Turn "I'm fine" into "I'm finally receiving support."

During your healing roller coaster, return to the Be stage as often as you want to. Conscious breath and centered stillness will allow you the time to stay present with your healing and stick with the process. You will begin to notice changes in your life, even if they are very small. Allow these changes to reinforce your trust in the process of healing.

Witness

Once you have found expression for your suppressed feelings and begun to let your instincts guide you, you are ready to move to neutral ground.

No matter where you are on the roller coaster of your healing crisis, you can step out of yourself and find a solid ground of objectivity that will allow you to observe what is happening, separate from your feelings.

This neutral ground is the home of your **witness**. Your witness is the inner observer of your life experiences. It is the part of you that can step back from the immediacy of what is happening and assume a viewpoint of absolute impartiality. The witness is the essence of you that is wise and loving. It functions from a warm glow of compassion that allows you to observe yourself without judgment or denial.

Your witness will be your trusted friend
and ally as you begin to heal.

Neutrality has magic in it. The neutral witness accepts whatever happens without judging or labeling it. The witness is present to support your feelings and help you see your experience clearly. When you begin to observe yourself through this lens of acceptance, you will shed a new light on your circumstances. This light will illuminate resources that allow healing to happen naturally and easily, leading you to solutions.

To engage your witness, take the following steps:

1. Close your eyes and take three full breaths.
2. Imagine that you are standing three feet away from your physical body.
3. Say aloud, "I invite my witness to observe my life, support my feelings, and increase my awareness of what I think, say, and do."
4. Look at yourself with the compassionate gaze of neutrality.

5. As you go about your day, notice how you are when you are alone, how you interact with others, and how you use your energy. Discover as much as you can about yourself, as if you were an alien trying to understand how humans live on earth. Be curious and nonjudgmental.

At the end of the day, share the witness's observations in your journal. From your standpoint three feet away from yourself, write impartially about what you observed. Stay focused on the crisis that you are healing, and be prepared for the possibility that your witness may observe a great amount of tension and negativity. Whether your observations are positive or negative, keep in mind that your witness is impartial and loving. Your witness would never judge you for what you feel, say, or do.

Examples of crisis observations might be:

"I just don't want to deal with the pain."

"The pain is in my right side all of the time it never stops stabbing me."

"I am emotionally crippled."

"I can't relieve the sick feeling in my gut."

"I need some time to rest and be alone."

"I am giving others people's opinions more strength than my own."

"I need help from my family."

"My crisis is allowing me to take time off from work."

"My life partner really showed that he/she cared."

Then, do the following:

- Read over what you have written and, through the neutral eyes of the witness, observe whether each statement is life-giving or life-draining. Is it life-draining to need help? Is it life-giving to notice how your crisis is affecting you? Write "life-giving" or "life-draining" next to each statement.

- Re-read your list and notice how you are responding to the world around you. What are your prevailing feelings and expressions? What are the circumstances that surround your daily life?

When you are in the depths of crisis, it can feel like your hands are tied and everything is life-draining. By supporting your feelings, your reactions and decisions shift to become life-giving rather than life-draining. You are redefining your life by being present with what you are feeling and experiencing. As you acknowledge your day from the point of view of the witness, you will begin to sort out what is negative and spontaneously move in a more positive direction.

As you engage with your witness, you are actually stepping beyond your crisis into a fresh perspective. Instead of standing at the epicenter of the storm, as you were in Be, you are now standing slightly outside the crisis, looking in.

Congratulations! You are now in a position to develop a relationship with healing that will move you into a positive future.

Chapter Four

Stay

How is it to witness yourself through your neutral inner eye?

As you move ahead to the next stage of healing, spend some more time cultivating your witness. Witnessing yourself with neutrality is a practice that will serve you well throughout your life. As you allow witnessing to become a natural part of how you move through each day, you develop the ability to see clearly how you are interacting with your world. Rather than judging and blaming how you are living, you will be able to state simply, "I am witnessing my day."

Witnessing allows you to stay with the feelings that arise without becoming attached to them. You can feel the feelings without being overcome. Witnessing allows your feelings to be a moment in time rather than becoming the story of your existence. Then, you can Be with the feeling without having it define who you are.

Witnessing allows you to experience feelings in three simple steps:

1. **Notice:** See what you are feeling.
2. **Acknowledge:** "I'm feeling this, and it's okay."
3. **Let go:** Release the feeling without having to act on it.

Witnessing gives you the power to stay present with the process of healing. This doesn't mean staying in a dangerous situation. It means staying present with yourself as you move through your crisis into healing. As you begin to heal, life will confront you with challenging situations that may tempt you to retreat. Retreat may feel safe, but really it will throw you back into the heart of your crisis. When you get the urge to retreat, it means transformation is near. Instead of retreating, stay. It is the power of staying that moves you through the challenges and into a better life.

The challenges you face are what we call your **confronting energy**— the events and reactions that occur around you. The confronting energy is your circumstances calling you out to pay attention and realize that you have power in your life. What you think and how you feel project outward onto the large movie screen that is your life. This projection is a direct representation of your internal world being mirrored back to you.

Your life is a mirror of your thoughts and feelings.

Life is confronting you through your crisis. Imagine your crisis as a good friend who has asked you to pay attention to your thoughts and feelings so that you can respond and make changes. This confronting energy can work with you and for you—and it won't go away. If you choose to avoid the confrontation now, it will show up again at another time. The circumstances may be different, but the confronting energy will be the same. The people and events around you will begin to respond to your suppressed feelings and act them out for you until you pay attention. For example, if you are embroiled in arguments with your spouse, they may intensify the more you repress your emotions.

In contrast, when you begin to understand and connect with the wisdom of your confronting energy, two things will happen: the intensity of your daily experience will diminish, and your pain will transform into positive feelings. For instance, the fights with your spouse may become less charged, allowing you to reconnect with what you love about him or her. As you continue to work with the confronting energy rather than resisting it, you will uncover the gifts hidden beneath the chaos of your crisis. You will find that life is an adventure that can be fun and enjoyable. You are ready to institute and witness positive change.

In Chapter Three, you started to define your feelings through the eyes of your witness. Now you can take it a step further and move through your confronting energy by engaging in a **reflective meditation**—a focused breathing exercise that helps you cut through the confusion and chaos of crisis and simplify what life is mirroring back to you. Reflective meditation will help you release your resistance to the confronting energy, allowing its source to appear. When you plug into the energy of the source, you can switch easily into positive living.

During your reflective meditation, you will concentrate one idea, thought, vision, word, or feeling until you gain new insight into your confronting energy. To begin your reflective meditation, choose a quiet time and read over the journal entries from Chapter Three. As you read what you wrote about your feelings, allow a significant word or phrase to pop out at you as if it's been highlighted. Hold the intention that what you choose will reveal something about your confronting energy. Don't think about it too much—just let your eyes be drawn there.

Alternatively, if you feel confident in your witness, you could close your eyes and ask the confronting energy to appear as a vision. Simply breathe, focusing your attention on your "third eye," located just above the bridge of your nose between your eyebrows. Then say, "Show me my confronting energy." Imagine the confronting energy being projected from your third eye.

Next, do the following meditation:

- Sit or lie down, close your eyes, and place your hands on your heart.
- Take a few deep, slow breaths.
- Picture the word or phrase you chose from your journal.
- Breathe into the word or phrase by focusing all of your energy on your third eye.
- Allow the word or phrase to expand and the boundaries to blur, as if the image were slightly out of focus.
- Push your energy into the vision, letting it grow larger and larger until it becomes uncomfortable.
- Stay with the discomfort until you feel it shift.
- Let go, and allow a new doorway to appear and open.
- Information will appear. Trust it.
- Remain still and silent, in a state of Be.

From this place of stillness and silence, describe in your journal what came up for you during your meditation. Stay with the description as long as possible to get in as many details as you can. Trust that your imagination is showing you an important truth.

Now, read over your description. This is the **base energy,** or energetic origin, of your crisis. Life has been confronting you with certain events and circumstances in response to the base energy. That's how powerful you are—the energy you hold within you creates what happens around you. Life takes energy, no matter what you are doing. You are an expert at using your energy; you don't even have to think about it. Going through a crisis uses a lot of your energy, and you have been doing it very well. Suffering takes a lot of energy. So does depression, anger, and pain.

It is essential to recognize and understand how you have been using your energy, and see that your life expression is based on a root cause. Seeing how you have been using your energy will allow you to shift its expression to more positive ends. By acknowledging your base energy, you can now claim your crisis as your own creation—then compassionately turn it around. At this crucial healing moment, it is very important to engage the neutral eyes of the witness so you can keep judgment, blame, shame, and guilt from stopping the process.

Positive movement begins with expression. If feelings aren't expressed, they will keep you stuck. Your base energy has a voice that has not yet been heard, and it has things to say. Some may be negative, and some may be positive. The first step is to let the base energy speak from the silenced voice of the negative. It is this silenced voice that has kept you stuck in crisis.

As if this silenced voice is a person, let it have its say, allowing it all the time and space it needs for expression. Speak from the depths of what you have discovered in your reflective meditation, giving it your full attention so that it can be recognized and heard.

Statement. As if "angry" were a person, let it speak. Speak out loud if you are in a safe place, or use your journal to write. If there is no voice, allow your breath to fill your hands and again invite the voice to speak.

Listen. Use your neutral inner ear to witness the voice of "angry." Allow the words to be real and heartfelt, without judgment or commentary. If judgmental voices come in, ask them to leave.

Be. When the voice is finished talking, let its energy dissipate by releasing your hands to your lap, palms up, and breathing deeply. Sit in Be.

How does it feel to release the negative voice that has been so powerfully running your life? Allow your witness to notice how you feel. Write in your journal about your experience.

When you are done listening, let go with your hands or put down your pen. Breathe in and out. Focus on your breath and let go of the words. After breathing, it is essential to move your body to help release the negative emotions. Dance around, go for a walk, or do whatever physical movement you can, with the intent to release stored emotion. The illustrated yoga posture is particularly effective.

Victory

Purpose: To release any remaining negativity and open your body to positive feelings for overcoming crisis.

Stand with your legs wide apart and knees bent, feet pointing to the side. Inhale, lifting your arms wide overhead. Exhale, sweeping your arms down and folding your torso forward. Repeat three to five times.

Be aware that the base energy might have more to say. Allow any further expression to come up over the next few days. Letting the base energy have its full say exhausts the potential for continuing down the negative path. By validating that the base energy is real, you create potential for a shift into the positive and spark a powerful new direction of positive living.

Continue to return to Be whenever you need to. It is important to keep nurturing yourself. You are going in to a deeper layer of self-expression that is critical for healing, and you need extra support.

PART THREE

live

Chapter Five

Stepping Out

Now that you have uncovered your confronting energy, defined your base energy, and given the negative a voice, you are ready to step fully into the positive energy of creation. You have dived deeply into your feelings, and now you can surface into a new level of living.

This may sound challenging, especially if you have been moving in and out of crisis for a long time. Yet it is far simpler than you may imagine. You have already found the base energy that has kept you stuck. Now, you will simply switch the circuits. Like flipping a light switch, you will learn how to switch the energy running your life from negative to positive.

Of course, like any new experience, stepping onto the positive path may sometimes feel awkward. It will take some time to acclimate, so go into BE whenever you need to. Be with yourself and Be gentle. You have lived in a crisis identity for an intense period, and it may take some time to recognize your new self.

Switching the Circuits

Now, here is the big secret to LIVE. It will propel you onto your positive path and start you moving toward what you want out of life. Are you ready?

The motivating energy of your life is positive.

No matter how negative things seem, you are always motivated by positive energy. This positive energy stems from your authentic life desires.

Take a few minutes to journal about what you really want out of life. Ask the question: **"Where do I want to be?"** Answer from a place of total spontaneity, without judging or censoring your desires. Allow yourself to feel the positive emotions that arise as you imagine your life just as you want it to be.

If this positive life hasn't been happening, it's not because something is wrong with you. It's simply that the negative energy has been blocking your way. With a light switch, the energy current is always there, right? All you need to do to turn the light on is flick the switch. Like the light switch, the energy of your desire is already there. All you need to do is flick the switch from negative to positive.

To begin the switch, you will picture two doors. The first door is the confronting energy of your crisis, such as the fights with your spouse. The second door is the **motivating energy** of your life. That motivating energy is usually very simple, such as, "I desire to be showered with love and affection."

Once you connect with your motivating energy, you can plug into the positive circuit instead of the negative. Switch from off to on. Go through the second door into infinite possibility. In this place of positivity, you are perfectly aligned to step forward on your authentic path. Life will begin to seem much easier when you can see this positive motivation and connect with its forward momentum.

Next, engage your witness and do the following meditation:

- Sit or lie down, close your eyes, and place your hands on your heart.

- Take a few deep, slow breaths.

- Picture two doorways, one behind the next.

- Engage your witness to be your guide through the doorways. Trust that the witness will take you through, without having to intellectually understand what is happening.

- Approach the first doorway. Notice that the defining word of your *confronting energy* is written on the doorway. Breathe deeply, open the door, and walk through.

- Close the door firmly behind you.

- Approach the second doorway. Pause in front of it and allow a word or phrase to appear on the door. Notice that it perfectly describes your *motivating energy*.

- Breathe into the word or phrase by focusing all of your energy on your third eye.

- Continue breathing, open the door, and walk through.
- Close the door behind you. Notice how it feels to be on the other side, in the full power of your motivating energy.
- Remain still and silent, in a state of Be.
- From this place of stillness and silence, accept the new vision and invite it to come into focus.
- Slowly open your eyes and write about it in your journal.

Body Communication

LIVE is where you literally *re-cognize* yourself—where you get to know yourself again, in the new light of the motivating energy. You now have the wonderful opportunity to say, "I am_____." This will be your affirmation —the redefinition of your circumstances exactly as you want them to be.

To connect with your affirmation, allow yourself to explore the mysterious being you call yourself. Who are you, apart from your crisis? What do you authentically want to express to the world? What do you want to share? How do you want to grow? To further discover who you are, let your motivating energy have the stage to speak by doing the following exercise:

- Inhale deeply through your nose. Exhale through your mouth, allowing yourself to voice a sigh of completion.
- Inhale again, inviting in the search for positive life flow and definition. Set the intention to listen for the positive voice, as if it has raised its hand and is awaiting its chance to speak.
- Acknowledge the raised hand by nodding and saying, "Go ahead, I'm ready to hear you now."
- Speak from the motivating energy and write what you hear in your journal.

Once you have heard from your motivating energy in detail, read over what you have written in your journal. Allow a word to jump out at you. This word is your **positive feeling**. Place your positive feeling into an "I am" statement: "I am _____." For example, "I am healthy" or "I am supported." This statement is your positive affirmation.

To complete this affirmation, do the following exercise:

Volcano Pose

Purpose: To harness the energy of positive affirmation.

Inhale, lifting your arms overhead. Say, "I am…" Exhale, bringing hands to heart. Finish with your positive feeling word, such as "supported." Repeat this sequence, increasing the vigor of your voice and movements until you feel like you are following your affirmation.

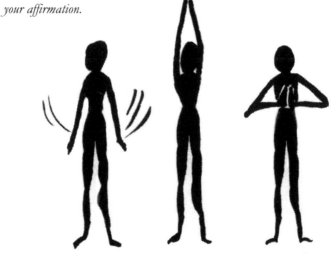

Your affirmation says to the world that you are open, present, and focused. To prepare yourself for taking positive steps, repeat the Pump from Chapter Two, incorporating your affirmation into the exercise.

Pump II

<u>Purpose</u>: To descend the energy of the affirmation deeply into your body, preparing you for taking action in Chapter Six.

Sit on your heels, or in a chair with your feet on the floor. Let your belly be soft and extended. Say your affirmation statement: "I am…" Inhale with relaxed belly then exhale actively, swiftly pulling up and in with your abdominal muscles. Repeat ten to twenty times.

*   *   *

If you are feeling challenged in accessing the positive, the next section will provide you with additional support.

It is important to be aware that the positive can come in the form of resistance. This is part of the process. Think of the resistance as the wrapping on the gift of your authentic desires. Trust that the right time will come to unwrap the gift.

To get ready to unwrap your gift, do the following exercise:

Walking Warrior

<u>Purpose</u>: To step forward in confidence, opening yourself to new opportunities

1. *From a standing posture, step out with your left leg. Turn your right toes out at a forty-five degree angle. Keep your hips and left foot pointing forward, arms at your sides.*
2. *Inhale and lift your arms around and out to the sides, lifting until they are overhead. Bend your left knee ninety degrees. Keep your right heel pressed to the ground.*
3. *Say, "I am stepping out."*
4. *Hold the position and breathe for up to three minutes.*
5. *Return to standing and repeat posture on the other side.*

You will know when it is time to unwrap your gift and move forward. At that time, go back into the previous exercise and create your positive affirmation.

Chapter Six

Living in the Now

Now that you have stepped into your positive affirmation, it is time notice what you are manifesting. Witness how powerfully you are inviting into your life people and events that respond to your positive energy. It is important to acknowledge that positive energy by taking time to integrate it. To integrate, employ the **Pause Factor**.

The Pause Factor is a simplified state of Be: one complete breath cycle, in and out. Use the Pause Factor to help you respond to the events and people in everyday life. By pausing and being present with what is happening, you can move from reaction into understanding. The Pause Factor gives you a moment of understanding before you respond to a situation.

This understanding opens the space for gratitude to enter. Gratitude is the foundation on which to build your positive new life. Gratitude is an essential component of forward growth and motion. Use the Pause Factor to help you cultivate a habit of gratitude. Notice the small positive events—the blessings that come to you throughout your day. Pause, then say "Thank you" and/or bow your head in a nod of acceptance.

Once you are grounded in gratitude, welcome the blessings that you are magnetizing. These blessings are the bricks that build your positive new life.

Simply recognizing and feeling gratitude for them places you on your life path.

To cement your blessings onto your positive path, enter a new, positive state of Be. Just as you used breath and journaling to Be with the authentic experience of your crisis, you can now use them to maintain a healthy state of Be as you move into your positive future. To focus your blessings into your positive path, do the following exercise:

Blessing Swirl

Purpose: To Be with your blessings, creating a path to your positive new life.

Sit on the floor cross-legged, or in a chair. Place your hands on your knees. Inhale and lift through the spine and crown of the head. Exhale, rolling your torso forward over your left knee, through center, over your right knee, then inhale back to center. As you swirl, focus through your third eye and see your life path taking form in front of you, noting the details. Repeat six to ten times.

When you have completed the swirl, write in your journal about the path you saw before you. Visualizing your path sets you on it. Now, you will be able to step easily into circumstances and relationships that support your positive life flow. We call this synchronicity.

Synchronicity happens when you are working with life instead of against it. Your power is turned on to believe you can achieve the positive, and your internal struggles resolve into the past. Synchronicity manifests in small or big "coincidences" that show up to help you, such as:

- The right person at the right time.
- The right information at the right time.
- The right situation at the right time.
- The right emotion at the right time.

Synchronicities connect you to positive people and events in ways that make life easy. Honor these synchronicities by taking action. If you meet the right person at the right time, say hello and follow through on the opportunity. This follow through is your honorary action. This action is a rite of passage into your new opportunities. It is what moves you forward on your path.

When you take an honorary action, you affirm to the world that you mean business and are committed to your new, positive life. Every action step allows you to let go and move into further integration with your positive path. As you move forward on your path, let go of the baggage you are carrying with you from the past. The more you let go of your past, the more completely you can fill yourself with a new sensation of positive life flow.

As you take more and more honorary actions, you will see that synchronicities appear like clockwork in your life. These synchronicities are opportunities. As opportunities show up, you will want to continually refine and redefine what it is that you want in order to get to your desired destination.

As you continue down your path, you will notice that the old, negative residue naturally fall away with ease and grace. New experiences and adventures will appear, challenging you to accept the bounty of life. Acceptance is seeing life through the lens of love. In a state of acceptance, you see everything as contributing to your well-being. If something throws you into negativity, employ the pause factor and accept it as a sign to help you maintain your positive flow.

To connect with acceptance, practice the following posture:

Acceptance Mudra

Purpose: To open yourself to new opportunities, new blessings and new beginnings.

Stand with your feet together, or two to three inches apart for balance. Push down through your toes. Lift through your legs and torso, straightening your spine and pushing through the crown of your head. With your arms by your side, open your palms to the front, extending through each finger, including your thumbs. Breathe deeply and say, either silently or aloud, "I am here. I am open. I am ready." Repeat the phrase several times. Return to the mudra as often as needed.

Write in your journal about acceptance. Notice what you are accepting that is new. See that acceptance can only happen in the present moment. This is where you need to be: right here, right now. It is time to leave the past behind.

That was then, this is now.

Then, you were suffering in the depths of crisis. *Now,* you are standing on your own two feet, moving into a new life of your own creation.

To plant your forward movement in the present, create a **positive declaration.** This is an "I am now living" statement that proclaims formally that you are in the vigorous stage of building a life you truly desire. It is the culmination of all the suffering you endured and all the healing you have done. By declaring to the world that you are healed, it becomes matter-of-fact. The action has been taken, and you embody the new beginning.

To create your positive declaration, do the following exercise:

Living from the Heart Moving Meditation

<u>Purpose</u>: To integrate the physical body with the spiritual, mental, and emotional shifts experienced through the previous exercises, and to clear the way for action.

Stand with feet together, or two to three inches apart for stability, or sit comfortably with a straight spine. With your arms straight down by your sides, state aloud, "I AM." Inhale and lift your arms overhead, bringing your hands together in prayer position. Bring your hands down to the third eye and say, "NOW LIVING." Bring your hands down to the heart and state, "FROM THE HEART." Push your hands all the way down to your sides to begin again. Repeat eight times, inserting your positive affirmation, such as: "I am now living from health." On the last round, push your hands all the way down to your sides then lift them up and out to the sides while saying, "YES!" Return to this exercise as often as you want to.

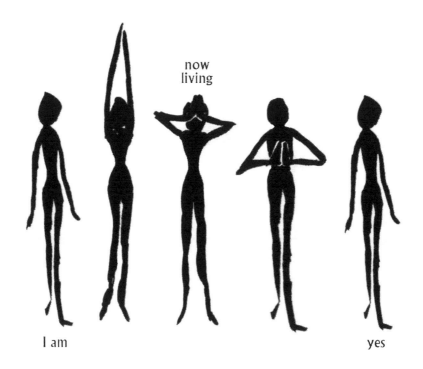

now
living

I am   yes

Saying "yes!" allows you to move forward and joyfully celebrate your heartfelt journey. Give yourself all the encouragement and acknowledgment that you deserve for daring to climb out of the depths of your crisis and begin anew on solid ground. You have given yourself the gift of clarity, and that gift will shine out into the world. Notice that as you change, the people and events around you shift, too. Watch closely as life aligns with your new sense of accomplishment. Note how easily life begins to fall into place. Be surprised by life and allow the surprise to fill your soul with joy.

Let life be your guide.

Appendix

Our unique **Seven Petals Technique** has been developing and evolving for many years. For more information on how Seven Petals can help you grow, expand, and transform, please visit our website at www.sevenpetalswellness.com.

We also wish to acknowledge the following techniques and ideas as instrumental in developing the Seven Petals Technique. We are grateful for the wisdom they have contributed. Please visit their websites for more information.

.

39364046R00035

Made in the USA
Charleston, SC
04 March 2015